HER STOLEN TEARS
RELEASE OF EMOTIONS

Daniella M. Butler

Her Stolen Tears
Release of Emotions
Daniella M. Butler

No part of this publication may be reproduced, distributed, or transmitted in any form or by any means, including photocopying, recording, or other electronic or mechanical methods, without the prior written permission of the publisher, except in the case of brief quotations embodied in critical reviews and certain other noncommercial uses permitted by copyright law. For permission requests, write to the author, addressed "Attention: Permissions" at info@daniellambutler.com.

Copyright © 2024 by Daniella Butler Trust
All rights reserved.

Butler, Daniella M.
Her Stolen Tears
www.DaniellaMButler.com
Email: info@daniellambutler.com

ISBN: 979-8-9921648-0-0 (Paperback)
ISBN: 979-8-9921648-1-7 (eBook)
ISBN: 979-8-9921648-2-4 (Hardcover)

Printed in the United States of America

First Edition: December 2024
Series: Unsilenced Voices

Contents

Shapes of Feelings, 1
My Stolen Tears, 2
A Little Girl Still Lives Inside of Me, 3
No Protection at Home, 4
Narcissist's Trophy, 5
Story of a Broken Arrow, 6
If He Loved You, 7
Judgment Unjust, 8
Life's Hourglass, 9

Missing You, 11
Waiting for My Daddy to Get Home, 12
Soon Come, My Child, 14
Big Brother Never Came Home, 16
A Life's Cycle, 18
Dear Mama, I Miss You, 21

Stolen Pieces of Self, 23
Stolen Gems, 24
My Stolen Audacity, 26
Soul's Agony, 28
The Angry Woman, 29

Cries of the Inner Victim, 31
The Cries of My Soul, 32
Body Paralyzed, 34
Lost In My Mind, 35
The Scars Within, 36
Crescent Moon on My Face, 38
My Pain on Loop, 39

Put a Bandage on My Pain, 40
Forced Forgiveness, 41
Incubator, 42
The Voice in My Sleep, 44
Predator's Prey, 45

Fight and Flight, 47
You're Not Good for Me, 48
The Shadow of My Past, 50
A Raging Storm Inside of Me, 51
Free Me from This Cell, 52
Shadowy Face I Could Not See, 54
The Queen Still Lives, 55

Frenemies and Foes, 57
Envy Is Friend, 58
The Monster's Words, 59
Forcing Feelings, 60
Protect Yourself, 61
No Military Protection, 62
Slandering the Victim, 63

Betrayal and Regret, 65
Unsaid Regret, 66
Visiting Regrets, 67
The Discarded Daughter, 68
Ashes of Betrayal, 70
No, No Regrets, 71

Reconstruction, 73
You Could Never Be Me, 74
Remnants of the Past Self, 76
Tears Turned Into Pearls, 77

This book is dedicated to the loving memory of my mother, Lillete.

Shapes of Feelings

My Stolen Tears

I
hide
my tears
deep inside
me where no
one can see. For
my heart can't bear
foreseen judgmental
stares from those who
claimed to love me. Love
that lasts to the end. A love
I do not believe. So, I hide my
tears away. But every time I hide
the torments lashed upon my soul,
my body slowly dies inside. Mentally, I
am not whole. I'm tired and weakened. I
can no longer endure these daily tortures
within my heart. So, it's time for me to leave.
For staying would mean the death of me. I no
longer produce new tears. They started drying
up long ago. I will no longer risk my life to stay.
With death closing in, I revealed my tears to all.
As foreseen, they stole some of my tears. With
pointing fingers and judgmental stares, their
words cut into my soul like a knife. To my
surprise, true loves revealed themselves
to me. Rushing in to protect my heart,
they stood by me as my angry soul
released its anguish. With their
love, I learned to let go of
My Stolen Tears.

A Little Girl Still Lives Inside of Me.

To the little girl inside of me,
I hope today you feel well-fed.
To the little girl inside of me,
I hope you feel no more dread.
To the little girl inside of me,
I hope the loneliness fades away,
To the little girl inside of me,
I hope this is a home for us to stay.
To the little girl inside of me,
I hope you can come out to play.
To the little girl inside of me,
I hope we don't have to run away.

Cradle me in your arms and protect me from the storm;
It's been viciously tormenting me since the age of ten.
She's crying, I'm crying for fear of being harmed,
A triggered memory on repeat with no end.

No Protection at Home

You protected me from enemies outside our walls,

Always ready to answer my calls.
I looked at you and said what was true,
Now who's going to protect me from you?
Those words tormented your sleeping nights,
Nightmare battles as you struggle with fistfights.
Fighting against your inner self to protect me,

In the end, your fist struck me.
Though you apologized to me,
I'm asking you to set me free.

For your demon that wakes up each morning
Has already shown my death in a forewarning.

Narcissist's Trophy

Your empathy is dead,
And your demons are fed.
You can't see through my eyes,
You look down on me with disdain.
Go ahead and put away the pretense;
In return, I will lower some of my defense.
Because there's nothing that I can say to you
To cause you and I to make any breakthroughs.

I remember when your words used to cut me like a knife.
After my epiphany, I realized you had no regard for my life.

You uplifted yourself up high and that is true,
Saying there are no beings as smart as you.
Your total arrogance is your shielded win,
Praising your narcissist self as you sing.

I strived for perfection,
Seeking your affection.
You are a manipulator,
I was your perpetrator.
I wanted to change you,
Evolution is me, not you.
Staying manifested pain,
And nothing was gained.

I remember when you won me with your *love;*
Silly me, I thought it was a blessing from above.

You uplifted yourself and that is true,
But there are no beings as pitiful as you.
Your total arrogance is your shielded win;
Heal your broken inner child when you sing.

Story of a Broken Arrow

You beat me with your words
That you drum in my brain,
Made me question myself
And lowered my self-worth.
You never laid a finger on me,
But your words were so much worse.
You see me as a broken arrow you can step on,
But these visions in my head tell me I'm much more.

You redefined me to the hate you wanted me to be,
Slowly stripping away layers of what I used to be.
You manipulated me with your hurtful words,
And then you happily smile at all my hurt.
You're unempathetic to my sorrows.
I don't expect you to say, "Sorry."
Broken arrow lost in your dirt,
Treated like I have no pain.

Always will be my fault;
I'm your hatred-love.
Won't stay in prison,
Escaping this hell.
The broken arrow
Lifted from dirt.

Pull bow back,
Aim up high.
Now shoot
To the sky.
Freedom,
I'm free!
A free,
Me.

If He Loved You

If he loved you,
Would you be sitting here all alone?
If he loved you,
Wouldn't he check on you from his phone?
If he loved you,
Would he continue to dismiss all your feelings?
If he loved you,
Wouldn't he be there while you were healing?
If he loved you,
Would he side with another person at first?
If he loved you,
Wouldn't he stop emptying your purse?
If he loved you,
Would he be on vacation without you?
If he loved you,
Wouldn't he get a job to pay bills too?
If he loved you,
Would he continue to make you cry?
He doesn't love you,
Wouldn't it be best to say goodbye?

This is what he wants to say:
"I do not love you in any way."

Judgment Unjust

Who do you think you are?
You oozing piece of human scar!
You have the nerve to be judging me?
After you freed him to descend upon me?

Where were you when he was bruising my skin?
Where were you when he was sinking his part within?
We know you released him because he looks like your kin.
You released him cause he's the reflection of your past sins.

For you deliberately dismissed my cries and pleads for help,
And now you're demanding I repent for defending myself?
Holding my head up high, I will accept your punishment.
Your justice is a lie that sleeps with your judgment.

Were you expecting me to feel some remorse?
To have some affection in my discourse?
I know exactly who the hell you are!
You oozing piece of human scar!

Life's Hourglass

Life begins—find a purpose that will keep you driven.

My mind lives in the present and the past,
Deciphering both as future forecasts.
Structuring my life like a psychic,
I give advice on paper encyclic.
With all my gained wisdom,
I still remained, "Victim."

Living my life in fear,
Encompassed in a sphere.
I use my wisdom as my crutch
And my children inherit each touch.
Engulfed by clarity in my twilight nights,
Sudden urge to fix wrongs as my end is in sight.

Life ends—you squandered the life that you were given.

Missing You

Waiting for My Daddy to Get Home

Waiting for my daddy on the front window seat;
Neighbors walked by, laughing and holding hands.
When Daddy gets home, he'll take me for a walk too.
I'll ride on his shoulders or be held in his arms,
Or he'll carry me by my tummy so I can fly up in the sky.
Oh, I just can't wait until my daddy gets home!

Mommy keeps saying, "Your daddy is not coming back."
I really wish she would just stop saying that!
My daddy said he would always be there for me.
He'll never leave me; he loves me and cares for me.
He'll show her! He'll never leave me when he gets home.
Oh, I just can't wait until my daddy gets home!

Waiting for my daddy on the front window seat,
Frowning—a short-haired girl pulled my hair at school today.
When Daddy gets home, I'll tell him all about it.
He'll go to my school and tell my teacher to spank her,
Or go to her house so her daddy can scold her.
Oh, I just can't wait until my daddy gets home!

Mommy keeps saying, "Your daddy is not coming back."
I really wish she would just stop saying that!
Sometimes my daddy gets home late from work,
Or he'll be sent far away to fight bad guys to save us.
He's just busy right now, but he'll come home to me.
Oh, I just can't wait until my daddy gets home!

Waiting for my daddy on the front window seat,
Looking at mommy with her humongous tummy.
When Daddy gets home, she'll stop eating so much.

He'll take us to the beach to have fun in the sun,
And we'll build a big sandcastle all the way up to the sky.
Oh, I just can't wait until my daddy gets home!

Mommy keeps crying, "Your daddy is not coming back!"
I really wish she would just stop saying that!
She combed my hair; I wore a pretty dress to church today.
We looked at a man in a coffin to say, "Goodbye."
Ready to go! I'll see Daddy when we get back.
Oh, I just can't wait until my daddy gets home!

Waiting for my daddy on the front window seat,
My mommy screamed out, "The baby is coming!"
Went to the hospital and *I'm a big sister now!*
Mommy said we gotta move—we can't stay in this house.
When Daddy gets home, he's gonna fix everything.
Oh, I just can't wait until my daddy gets home!

I asked Mommy, "When is my daddy coming home?"
She drew me close to her, kissed me, and held me tight.
She said, "You told him goodbye; he's in Heaven now."
He didn't look like Daddy; please stop saying that!
I ran to the window seat to wait for my daddy.
Crying and waiting, but my daddy never came home.

Soon Come, My Child

My heart broke within my chest
As I laid my child to rest.
Consumed by sorrow and grief
As I sank in disbelief.
How must I live without You?
This can't be real; it's not true.

IT SHOULD HAVE BEEN ME INSTEAD!
IT SHOULD HAVE BEEN ME WHO'S DEAD!

"Soon come," whispered in her ear.
"Soon come," for my time is near.

Felt like my heart was in exile.
Everything I touched was vile.
My anger for God compiled.
NO, PLEASE GIVE ME BACK MY CHILD!
How should I live without You?
Please be lies; it can't be true.

IT SHOULD HAVE BEEN ME INSTEAD!
IT SHOULD HAVE BEEN ME WHO'S DEAD!

"Soon come," whispered in her ear.
"Soon come," for this time I'm near.

Oh, I want to kiss your face
As my tickles make you brace.
Clasp your face between my hands,
Slip through my fingers like white sand.
How can I live without You?
I don't want it to be true.

IT SHOULD HAVE BEEN ME INSTEAD!
IT SHOULD HAVE BEEN ME WHO'S DEAD!

"Soon come," whispered in her ear.
"Soon come," for my time draws near.

Lying awake thinking of you,
Wishing this nightmare was not true.
Pain that recycled to new,
A world with me and no *you*.
Life may go on without you,
But my heart will carry you.

I wished it was me instead!
But my heart knew you were dead.

"Soon come," whispered in her ear.
"Soon come," wait for me, my dear.

Big Brother Never Came Home

I closed my eyes and saw your face:
You were dying in a dreadful place.
You were my brother and childhood friend,
This should have never been your end.
Big brother, you never came home,
But that monster is FREE TO ROAM!

Childhood memories in my head,
I still can't believe you are dead.

Every time that I closed my eyes,
I saw your death and heard your cries.
Your hand reached out to touch mine,
Through distant places across time.
Big brother, you never came home,
But that monster is FREE TO ROAM!

Childhood memories in my heart,
I will never let them depart.

I closed my eyes and asked God why
Your gentle soul had to die.
Wrong place, wrong time; he took your life,
Heartless SOUL who kills with a knife!
Big brother, you never came home,
But that monster is FREE TO ROAM!

Childhood memories in my soul,
I will cherish them as my goal.

Every time that I closed my eyes,
I felt you fading with the skies.
All your hopes and dreams have vanished,
That Monster's SOUL should be BANISHED!
Big brother, you never came home,
That monster's end is IN DEATH'S TOME!

A Life's Cycle

I remember summer kisses,
The comfort of your warm embrace,
As our dreams turned into wishes,
Pressing against your handsome face.
Our laughter turned into stitches,
A permanent part of your space,
Overwhelming joy like riches,
I soar and I run with your pace.

Sky above me,
Prayers sent high.
Earth below me,
Wondering why.

Our faces were always smiling,
Your touch puts me into a trance.
As one, our bodies were bracing,
In love with your hypnotic glance.
Body heat continued rising,
Making love, the spiritual dance.
No fear of love compromising,
United from a happy chance.

Sky above me,
Prayers sent high.
Earth below me,
Wondering why.

Entrusted with a blessed seed,
Little fingers held with soft grasp.
After entrance of joyful deed,
Wrapped in a blanket like a clasp.

Listening to stories I read,
One character's voice became rasp.
Love's moment where happiness breathes,
I felt protection from the asp.

Sky above me,
Prayers sent high.
Earth below me,
Wondering why.

Sightseeing while driving places,
Teasing each other type of fun.
The warmth from the happy faces,
We enjoyed the beautiful sun.
Worried by the winter traces,
Hearts panic as our tires run,
Silence and motionless faces,
An end that cannot be undone.

Sky above me,
Prayers sent high.
Earth below me,
Wondering why.

I emerged in funeral black,
The anger in my heart won't die,
Braced as my heart began to crack,
I'm crying as I asked God *why*,
Begging him to *BRING THEM BACK!*
Without them, my insides have died,
Broken, my life falls off the tracks,
NO, not ready to say goodbye!

Sky above me,
Prayers sent high.
Earth below me,
Wondering why.

My family taken from me,
Must find a purpose for this wrong,
Tell me, has God forsaken me?
Poured my sorrow in a love song,
My revealed purpose, I now see,
Helping others now makes me strong,
Last mission of love's final key.

Dear Mama, I Miss You

Dear Mama,

I'm writing you this letter to let you know that I'm feeling much better. I wanted you to know that I'm finally free. Yeah, just like you thought I ought to be. My first thought was of you and all the pain you saw me go through. Your words were never wasted; they helped me through some dark spaces.

Mama, I remember the day I first became a mother. Giving birth to my own child was a feeling like no other. Mama, I understand, and I appreciate your guiding hand. Just know that I'm never going back to that prison, where I spent most of my life without living. I know it's been more than 10 years since I last saw your face, so I'm coming to visit you for guiding grace.

While on my way to visit you, I decided to visit the old house too. It's now older and worn, but partially reborn. I waited patiently for the owner to emerge, and I watched as she made her stand beside the verge. Unsurprisingly, we stared at each other decisively. Merged into one, I now drive to you in the high sun.

Mama, I miss your smile and your warm embrace. You felt like home to me like no other place. I apologize for not visiting you sooner, but the fear of you not hugging me felt like a tumor. All the years of selfless love is now an entity in the sky above. The last time I saw your beautiful face was when we said goodbye at your final resting place.

Stolen Pieces of Self

Stolen Gems

My home is now damaged,
Was forced in and ravaged.
My front door kicked in,
Showing signs of the sin.
A precious gem now removed
Was once sealed and unused.
Stolen gems now gone forever,
Glass cover of missing lever.

No pictures on the walls,
Shattered pieces in the halls.
Books pulled from every shelf,
Ripped pages of the self.
Broken dishes on the floor,
Holes bashed in every door.
Stolen gems now gone forever,
Glass cover of missing lever.

Every wall clawed with red,
Roof scraps missed my head.
Broken windows bring forth stares;
My face leaks shameful tears.
Overwhelmed by all the damage,
Mended pieces from the baggage.
Stolen gems now gone forever,
Glass cover of missing lever.

My pain now deemed invalid,
Deprived of my soul's allod.
Thief is now the victim,
Wants amnesty from the condiction.
Beautiful outwardly but disgusting within,
Never atoning for his sin.
Stolen gems now gone forever,
Glass cover of missing lever.

My walls crumbling around me,
My screams trapped inside me.
Yearned for a safe place,
Instead removed myself from trace.
Can't undo all the damage,
What you did was savage.
Stolen gems now gone forever,
Glass cover of missing lever.

My Stolen Audacity

I was young and I was naive;
My youth gave me no reprieve.
You began to groom my childhood years
As your older hand wiped away my tears.

So, it took me a minute,
Because I was embedded within it.
But little by little I started to realize,
That you are indeed a demon in disguise.

Oh, the audacity of me!
For thinking you truly cared about me!
Go ahead and continue to set yourself free;
I guess this is how my life was meant to be.

You played with the purity of my youth;
My naivety couldn't decipher the truth.
And now my belly swells yet again;
Judgement makes me feel my life should end.

Busybodies discussing my life's worth;
I guess I should have pre-knowledge at my birth.
Pretending they made no mistakes in their youth;
Erasing and rewriting their history's truth.

Oh, the audacity of me!
How dare I be born experience-free!
Go ahead and keep on judging me;
I already feel like my life wasn't meant to be.

Little faces that came from my womb,
For them, I will not prematurely go to my tomb.
We deserve a life filled with happiness;
Not this void overwhelmed with emptiness.

Gossipers insisting my life is ruined,
Like the crumbling remains of ancient ruins.
Saying no man will want a young woman like me;
A consensus they all gathered to agree.

Oh, the audacity of me!
For wanting a happy ending for me!
I overcame a lot to be the woman you now see;
A worthy battle to set my soul free.

Soul's Agony

What you took
Did not belong to you.
What you took
Was not your own.
But like a thief,
You take from others,
And like a thief,
You're a filthy hole.
What you did
Was meant to conquer me.
What you did
Destroyed my soul.
In the end,
I chose my final breath.
Before my end,
I avenged my soul.

Beneath the ground,
I'm free from agony.
Rest in peace
To my soul.

The Angry Woman

A howling wind blew through my soul,
Taking with it all my warmth and glow.
The chill of it shivered down my spine,
Forcing a replay of my misery over time.
The hatred and anguish painted on my face
Tells a story I wish with all my heart, I could erase.

The universe continually moves on;
The sun will always rise after dawn.
Time will never stop for my misery;
Taking on burdens is life's trickery.

The reflection I now see in the mirror is of a stranger.
Where's the me that escaped imminent danger?
Looking at me I see the remnants after death,
A shadowed self after regaining my breath.
No more innocence or sweet femininity,
Revenge required a different ability.

My youthful vigor is devoured and replaced.
Instead, an angry woman is now in its place.
My misery became intertwined with reality,
And now my anger has become my true sanity.

Cries of the Inner Victim

The Cries of My Soul

Seasons of treasons upon my soul,
Buried beneath my unchosen role.
Emerged in this lifelong script,
A foreseen ending of death's crypt.

MY MIND CAN'T TAKE THIS ANYMORE!
I must escape through any open door!
Why must I continue this dance?
Like a zombie stuck in a trance.

I was told to go on living,
That life's a gift that keeps on giving.
With lifeless limbs and a muted voice,
Must I continue this life without any choice?

MY HEART CAN'T TAKE THIS ANYMORE!
Making me pulsate on the dirty floor!
Why must I keep on singing?
Like a caged bird with anxiety swinging.

Seasons of treasons upon my soul,
Too many holes to make me whole.
Carry me away to another plane,
Reincarnate me without any chains.

MY BODY CAN'T TAKE THIS ANYMORE!
Not sitting around to wait for a cure!
Why must my heart keep on beating?
An inner voice said failure means repeating.

I was told to learn life's lessons,
Otherwise, I'll restrict all my blessings.
That I too am a beautiful treasure,
That blooms when focused on my pleasure.

But my soul can't take this anymore!
My humanity is beaten and sore!
Why must I continue this fight?
My inner voice says to do what is right.

Body Paralyzed

My mouth is wide open,
My screams are unspoken.
My volume is muted,
My voice box is looted.
All sounds released from me!
Cause no one can hear me!

My body paralyzed,
Fear of death and demise.
Struggling, motionless,
Picture of hopelessness.
Heart pounding in my chest!
Is this my final test?

Dear Lord, can you hear me?
I lay and pray to thee.
Give me another chance!
Wake me up from this trance!
Waiting here patiently,
My mind drifts aimlessly.

Anxiety released,
I accept my disseized.
Drift my thoughts to the skies,
Relax then close my eyes.
Hear the sound of my breath!
Thank the Lord for no death!

My body gained freedom!
Run free with new wisdom!
Tread carefully in fear,
My new prison is clear.
Close eyes and meditate,
For time will heal my faith.

Lost in the Mist of My Mind

I'm lost in the mist of the fog in my mind,
Air so thick I'm hard for you to find.
I hear voices speaking in the mist,
They keep telling me to stop, to cease to exist.
But in the distance, I hear you telling me to resist.

I'm lost in the mist of the fog in my mind,
Waiting for someone to send me a sign.
Is this a dream or is this reality?
Please tell me I'm not losing my sanity.
But in the distance, you tell me to wait for clarity.

I'm lost in the mist of the fog in my mind,
Unable to count the elapsing of time.
My body aches from pain I cannot see,
Will I wither away while everyone abandons me?
But in the distance, you promise you'll stay with me.

I'm lost in the mist of the fog in my mind,
Suddenly, I remembered I was a victim of a crime.
My eyes moistened at the vast nothingness,
A prison created from my own subconsciousness.
In the distance, you vow to fill my heart's emptiness.

I'm lost in the mist of the fog of my mind,
It's finally fading, I'm no longer blind.
As the sweet breeze blows, the fog begins to clear,
Your smell engulfs me, as your smiling face appears.
You tell me, "It's time to go home my dear."

The Scars Within

Mirror reflection of scars on my face,
Attempting to cover with piled-on paste.
Constant reminder of wrong that was done,
Hiding my face from the light of the sun.
Enclosed in my shell locked with a lost key,
Beyond the surface is where you'll find me.

The tattered book that no one will open,
Siege of my voice becoming unspoken.
Judged, condemned to stay hidden on the shelf,
Back of the library—my archived self.
Enclosed in my shell locked with a lost key,
Beyond the surface is where you'll find me.

DISFIGURED, DEFORMED, REGARDED EVIL!
The words of the beautiful medieval.
Ugly within but angelic outside,
Their voices are heard and mine pushed aside.
Enclosed in my shell locked with a lost key,
Beyond the surface is where you'll find me.

SHAKEN AND RAGED, WHAT'S BECOMING OF ME?
Will I become the monster that they see?
Constant beatings by the words of their tongue!
No protection from the fun of their young!
Enclosed in my shell locked with a lost key,
Beyond the surface is where you'll find me.

The future is still a mystery to me,
My heart tells me I deserve to be free!
FREE OF HATRED FROM "BEAUTIFUL FACES,"
Sometimes I want to put them in cases.

Enclosed in my shell locked with a lost key,
Beyond the surface is where you'll find me.

"LISTEN," the loudest voice yelled, "KILL YOURSELF!"
Standing tall, laughing, and proud of herself.
Alone, no voices will stand up for me,
Exhale, my future is now clear to ME.
Enclosed in my shell locked with a found key,
Beyond the surface is where you'll find me.

Crescent Moon on My Face

Crescent moon on my face,
A scar your fingernail did trace.
When I see this crescent moon,
I'm reminded of that day in June.

Arguing in the driving car,
Your anger left me with a scar.
Our children in the backseat,
Watching their mommy's defeat.

For I married such a man;
Attacking his driving wife was his plan.
When your anger leads to a crime,
You justify it each and every time.

For I swerved on an empty road,
Curing your venomous mouth as we drove.
But your anger swelled yet again;
You became a demon in the end.

Talking to you is in vain,
Your anger is indeed insane.
Digging firmly into my flesh,
You left a crescent moon I detest.

Letting go of my flesh,
The wound bled red; it was fresh.
Crescent moon on my face,
A scar your fingernail did trace.

You took the children in the house.
In the car, I wished I had no spouse.
You emerged and saw the bloody trace.
Then asked, "You did that to your face?"

My Pain on Loop

As I lay motionlessly in my bed,
A video keeps playing in my head.
A horrid crime that happened long ago
Has held me captive, unable to grow.
Scenes from the sin play on constant repeat,
Pinpointing the moments of my every defeat.
A constant battle to siege my mind,
I wonder if this punishment was assigned?

Telling me what you would have done
In a tragedy you have never run.
Oh, does that make you feel empowered?
Wow, you're judging me like a coward.
Have you walked footsteps of my life?
Stop cutting me with your dirty knife.
Said what someone else would have done,
Uplifting another while treating me like scum.

Triggered from the sounds of the weather.
Triggered by the sounds of lovers' pleasure.
Triggered from the memories of the sin.
Triggered by the torments that dwell within.
Trapped by thoughts created in my mind.
Traumatized while waiting for a safe sign.
Take these videos out of my head.
They're turning me into the walking dead.

Put a Bandage on My Pain

Put the bandage on my pain
As my face begins to rain.
Put the bandage on my hopes
While I untie these heart ropes.

My mood, like a metronome,
Is going back and then forth.
My moods hit with a firm cling,
Ball of a pendulum swing.

Is my pain annoying you?
Has my anguish changed your view?
I sought refuge in your home,
But my pain harshens your tone.

Oh, so grief has time limits?
I exceeded those digits?
I must only trust in you?
When will my ramblings be through?

Solitude is my best friend
That has no condition's end.
It's now my sacred safe place,
Always allowing me grace.

Forced Forgiveness

Forgiveness is mine alone to give.
It was never yours to demand at will.
Your empty apology breathes insincerity.
A forced forgiveness will not be given,
For you lost all your control over me.

A smiling face told me that I must forgive.
She said forgiveness is for me and not for him.
Saying that if I don't forgive, I'm holding onto sin.
I need you to stop trying to control my free will,
For I clearly did not ask you for your advice.

It's said forgiveness doesn't mean you will forget.
Yes, it cannot erase the night terrors he carefully left.
My forgiveness is given to ignorant and innocent minds.
So, please, allow me to heal without invading my space.
Letting go and forgiveness have different meanings.

Incubator

Like a thief in the night, you were gone;
You impregnated me before dawn.
You planted a seed with no responsibility
While running off in the night with my virginity.
You took it away without my permission,
Woke up to find you accomplishing your mission.
With your innocent face, who would believe me?
In their eyes, you couldn't deceive me.

My body has now been confiscated,
Forced against my will to feel obligated.
With my rights waived as the victim,
I've become an incubator in this system.

Results warned of an unsafe pregnancy,
The chance of his death was a high expectancy.
Being raped and now carrying a dying child,
I ripped at my skin for being defiled.
I writhed in agony as I groaned,
For my life had become the Twilight Zone.
And after a failed attempt at taking my life,
They shackled my hands and took my knife.

My body is completely under surveillance,
Stripped of its rights with the system's valence.
My decision was denied and deemed vile,
For I wanted to release a dying child.

As I assume my role as the incubator,
Everyone feels blessed for being the instigator.
With joyful smiles for making decisions for me,
Complications arise and my soul is set free.
His shallow breathing is his first breath,
And my body is now released to its death.
His short tragic life marks the end of mine,
Which of us is the victim this time?

The Voice in My Sleep

As I lay asleep on our bed,
A breath came closer to my head.
Telling me the bad things you've said
And that I really should be dead.

"No one loves you;
No one here cares.
They all wished you
Would disappear."

As I lay asleep on our couch,
A voice said, "You're a lazy slouch."
The breathing lowers to a crouch,
Then covers my head with a pouch.

"No one loves you,
No one near cares.
They all wished you
Would disappear."

I opened my eyes with a scream;
Jumping up from night terror dreams.
Looking at my wrist at the seam,
Fighting with thoughts as my tears streamed.

"No one loves you,
No one there cares.
They all wished you
Would disappear."

Predator's Prey

The anguish of your tortured soul
Has developed jealousy holes.
As inner victim starts to prey,
Your angry soul begins to stray!

YOU ARE CONSUMED BY YOUR ANGER,
YOU'RE BECOMING A VILE CANCER,
YOU FIND JOY IN INFLICTING PAIN,
YOUR BLOOD PULSES HATE THROUGH ITS VEINS!

No longer a victim that mourns,
Your true predator self is born.
Your innocent cries have vanished;
You now cry in monster's anguish!

LOOK, your mirror can now reflect
What your soul already detects:
The true evil you once detest
Is now residing within your chest!

Fight and Flight

You're Not Good for Me

My momma told me you're not good for me,
Didn't listen; thought I could set you free.
I said I love you, you'll be good to me,
But in the end, you caged me and hid the key.

Consumed by words, you beat into my face,
Cause you have to make sure I know my place.
Never have I doubted your cold embrace,
Or your threats of removing me from trace.
Nightmares, with shadows, holding me in place,
Telling me I'm a waste of all your space.

My momma told me you're not good for me,
Didn't listen; thought I could set you free.
I said I love you, you'll be good to me,
But in the end, you caged me and hid the key.

Worried about what the neighbors might think,
Telling my family might bring me to drink.
Laughter from people wanting me to sink,
My anxiety is making me shrink.
Running away, I'm starting to rethink,
I'm trying to hold on, to my last brink.

My momma told me you're not good for me,
Didn't listen; thought I could set you free.
I said I love you, you'll be good to me,
But in the end, you caged me and lost the key.

Walking away, leaving your ass behind,
I don't need your permission; I resigned.
Never your equal, just someone to grind;
Wow, you even tried to control my mind.
Don't know where I'm going, I'm driving blind,
Feeling lost, but it's myself I must find.

My momma told me you're not good for me,
Didn't listen; thought I could set you free.
I said I love you, you'll be good to me,
In the end, you caged me, but I stole the key.

The Shadow of My Past

The shadow of my past is chasing me;
I hid in a place where she could not see.
In this magical place where I now dwell,
Neither my pain nor sorrow can excel.

The shadow of my past is chasing me;
When will she just let go and set me free?
Bringing with her memories lost long ago,
Memories that should be buried and not sown.

The shadow of my past is chasing me,
Causing cracks in my world where I can see.
In this world, I have built my perfect home,
But she's attacking my protective dome.

The shadow of my past is chasing me;
From her persistent grasp, I must now flee.
For she broke into my protected cell,
Bringing with her memories of my past hell.

The shadow of my past is chasing me;
She's now standing tall right in front of me.
Forcing me to accept my painful past,
She destroyed my home with a spell she cast.

The shadow of my past is chasing me,
Playing memories I did not want to see.
Bitter tears began to invade my face,
As I fell to the floor and screamed in place.

A Raging Storm Inside of Me

There's a storm brewing deep inside of me,
Beckoning, demanding to be set free.
Seven years of you causing torment upon my skin,
Has built a raging storm that dwells within.

You hesitate before drawing near,
Always attacking me from the rear,
Knocking me out because you know I'll fight back,
As I feed our children before your sneak attack.

I'm warning you, don't cause me any more pain,
Or this storm will descend upon you while assuming her rein.
Her release will mean the eradication of you,
There's no re-closing this door once she comes through.

I told my children, "Goodbye for now,
I will come back for you and that is my vow.
For if I stay, your father will be dead,
And then your mother will be in prison instead."

Seven years of not being a full-time mother,
I finally built a life to protect my children from others.
You asked for forgiveness and to start anew.
I carefully listed all the pain you put me through.

I'm warning you, remove your hand from my shoulder,
The hospital will be your home if you continue to get bolder.
I could no longer suppress the raging storm within,
You pissed her off—now atone for your sin.

Free Me from This Cell

Listen to my heart
That beats within my soul.
Can you hear my cries for help
Within this filthy cell?

Help me steal the key.
It's hanging on the wall.
First, climb down in the well,
Where a secret dungeon dwells.

Free me from this cell!
Free me from this hell!
I WANT TO BE SET FREE,
RETURNING BACK TO ME!

Free me from this cell!
Where no one should dwell!
I WANT TO SOAR UP HIGH,
ABOVE THE PAINTED SKY!

Listen to my heart
That's deep within my soul.
While descending down the well,
Cast protection on yourself.

Help me to escape.
Pass the guard outside the gate.
Now go and grab the key,
Then set my soul free.

Free me from this cell!
Free me from his spell!
I'M READY FOR THE FIGHT,
BUT FIRST I MUST TAKE FLIGHT!

Free me from this cell!
His dark heart still dwells!
I WANT TO LIVE MY LIFE,
WITHOUT THE PAIN AND STRIFE!

Listen to my heart
That lives within my soul.
Now it's time to do my part;
I trapped the monster in the well.

Since you helped me to escape,
I'll bestow this magic cape.
But you can't retrap my heart;
You knew this from the start.

Shadowy Face I Could Not See

Shadowy face I could not see,
I'm coming to face my destiny.
You hide in a space plain in sight,
Waiting for our future fight.

I know I still feel fear
As I approach you near.
It's something I can't hide,
Not buried deep inside.

Shadowy face I could not see,
I'm coming to face my destiny.
You tortured me for too long;
Shadowy face, you should be gone.

I know I must be brave
While entering your cave.
It's obvious to see,
But I will never flee.

Shadowy face I could not see,
I'm coming to face my destiny.
Whether I live or if I die,
It's time for us to say goodbye.

The Queen Still Lives

I'm a motherless child,
I'm half an orphan.
The queen is dead,
Now I'm a crownless princess.

You can't see my worth,
You think I'm an easy prey.
And since the lioness is not around,
You torture me mercilessly every day.

But the queen is not dead,
For you see, she resides inside of me.
And as I grow and endure your torture,
Eventually, I will become what I was meant to be.

All the years of abuse you have inflicted
Will be given back to you tenfold with conviction,
For I was born to become the queen.
You cannot destroy the essence which is me.

Frenemies and Foes

Envy Is Friend

My victories became your fuel
For hate and competitive duels.
My happiness is your sadness
And my sorrow brings you gladness.
Sabotage is your sacred tool
That you used to make me your fool.

Envious heart beats in your chest;
I will not be your final quest.

I trusted in your love for me.
That was a trap I did not see.
You pretended to be my friend;
My destruction was your goal's end.
Remove the mask you hide behind;
I should have foreseen all your signs.

Envious heart beats in your chest;
I know I'm not your final quest.

Hollow words spewing from your mouth
Before your lies descended south.
Blaming everyone but yourself
Used to cause me to doubt myself.
The only thing I wanted from you
Was your acceptance of what is true.

Envious heart beats in your chest,
Now you're looking for a new quest.

The Monster's Words

"Stop making me out to be a monster,"
Words you use to make yourself the victim.
"Let it go, it's all in the past,"
Words you use to deflect all my pain.
"Why can't you get over it?"
Words you use to dismiss me.
"I was young, and I made a mistake,"
Words you use that show no regret.

"Quit being a victim,"
Words you use to silence my voice.
"That's not how I see it,"
Words you use to distort your actions.
"I'm sorry *you* feel that way,"
Words you use to say you don't care.
"Are you sure you're remembering it correctly?"
Words you use to gaslight me.

"I'm a good person,"
Words you use to lie to yourself.
"You're not perfect,"
Words you use to manipulate me.
"You made me do it,"
Words you use to shift all the blame.
"You're the problem, not me,"
Words you use that prove you're a monster.

Forcing Feelings

I finally understand this selfish man
Who's angry with me for ruining his plan.
How dare I have no feelings for him?
No feelings for him, he perceives as a sin.
To him, my emotions are irrelevant.
His wants for me are more prevalent.

Calling me all sorts of nasty names
To manipulate me with his brazen games.
Disrespecting my entire ancestral strain;
Not wanting him means I must feel pain.

I'm not taking responsibility for your feelings,
You and I are different entities with no dealings.
Not selling my soul because you want to bed me;
My feelings won't change even if you want to wed me.
Listen, I've already respectfully declined,
Should I explain how harassment is defined?

Calling me all these despicable names,
Manipulatively playing these shameful games.
You can't force feelings that don't exist,
Quit attacking me and cease to persist.

What is wrong with this belligerent man?
He needs to go to radiology for a brain scan.
Help him find a therapist to sort out his feelings,
Maybe after that, he'll begin his journey to healing.
Do I need a restraining order for him to keep his distance?
Because his mental health is a threat to my existence.

Protect Yourself

Protect your heart,
Protect your soul.
Protect the pieces
That make you whole.

You work so hard
From dusk till dawn.
Ungrateful people
See you as a pawn.

The universe won't wait for you.
The universe won't stand still.
For the universe will go on,
Even when you are gone.

Now dry your eyes,
Stand up, be strong,
You are the daughter
Of a love composed.

No one's above you
Like no one's below.
Don't let their hatred
Wound your soul.

No Military Protection

She joined the military proudly
And her parents cheered her on loudly.
She thought everyone was equal and all the same,
But her military experiences taught her that was insane.

For ever since a military predator destroyed her core,
Her military service will protect her no more.
For they sent him away to another base
And saved his career by having no rape case.

Although her male friends kicked his ass,
His military protection rewarded him with a career pass.
He gets future retirement, and she gets urgency to move on,
But with a PTSD diagnosis, her career is basically gone.

It seems the military neglects the female gender,
Low rating VA disability chump change is the render.
So many victims with no military protection as a backstory;
Is this what you call honor and glory?

Slandering the Victim

Dear foes,

Please stop blaming victims for their woes. You're judging her for not dressing like a saint around perverts with no restraint. It doesn't matter what she wears. Perverts can appear anywhere.

Instead, how about you do us a favor? Teach your sons better behaviors. Tell him to keep his hands and parts to himself and to find someone who wants his evil self. Please stop filling their heads with excuses and giving them justification for their abuses.

Why are you behaving like a vulture and uplifting the rape culture? That mentality is truly disgusting because it blames victims for predators lusting. Then when the same thing happens to a loved one or you, you cry when the same judgment is placed on you.

You're going around toting your opinions as being realistic. Don't you know the predator's action is sadistic? You're sitting on a pedestal slandering the victim. It's like you think you're the final judge, stating your dictum. I can't control foes or predators' minds, but the fact still remains that the predator committed the crime.

Betrayal and Regret

Unsaid Regret

"I can't unsay the hurtful words I've said
Or remove those memories from your head.
I can't unsee your tear-filled eyes
Or soothe the hurt I've caused with all my lies.
I can't unhear the sadness in your voice
Or reverse time to remove me as your choice.
I can't undo the pain I've inflicted
Or pretend that it never existed.

I pray that you can forgive me with time.
I *regret* you'll never again be mine."

Beautiful words that remain unsaid,
Dream-filled scene that dwelled in my head.
My past with you can never be undone
Or visions of you hurting me for fun.
Stripping away your essence as I undress,
I realize this is one of life's wicked tests.
Closure will come when we're both unalive.
I shift my focus so my soul can revive.

I will never forgive you at any moment in time.
I *regret* the day I ever thought you were mine.

Visiting Regrets

A life that's no longer meant to be
Often visits me at my door,
Showing me what could have been,
A life I would have adored.
But reality slapped me across the face
And showed me my current state.
For I was tricked into taking his path
And now I'm stuck in this treacherous place.

The Discarded Daughter

You said I'm nothing but a mere little girl
Who's groomed to be a rich man's pearl.
For your son will inherit your legacy
And I will be sold for my celibacy.

For what can a little girl like I do?
Constantly viewed as a liability by you.
Thank you for the sperm that gave me life,
But you do not decide to whom I will be wife.

I endured your berating of psychological abuse.
Trust I will put these experiences to good use.
Mental record of attacks against my skin
And telling me that I could never win.

I ran away to further my education;
I will no longer suppress my indignation.
Selling me to an old man is not part of my plan,
For my destiny has always remained in my hand.

In time you gave your fortune to your dearest son,
Now look, he's squandering it and having fun.
He's causing chaos and ruining your name;
Is this your legendary family's fame?

I worked tirelessly to secure my faith,
Now you pretend to be my fatherly saint.
I will not allow you to take credit for my rise;
You left me desolated after cutting family ties.

With a spoiled son and a discarded daughter,
Who's taking care of you, my aging father?
When heaven called my mother home,
Your son left you in a nursing home.

So, what the hell is in your name?
Don't your blood run through my veins?
You decided to discard me like I was trash,
Now that I've risen you demand parental cash.

Shameless father chastises discarded daughter,
Where's your precious son, my dearest father?
When I became homeless after your abuse,
I promised, you would regret your deuce.

Ashes of Betrayal

From the ashes of betrayal
Comes an overflow of tears and regret.
From the ashes of betrayal
Comes my angry woman stares and sighs.
From the ashes of betrayal
Comes repeat memories asking myself, why?
From the ashes of betrayal
Comes the reveal of real friends and love.
From the ashes of betrayal
Comes judgment from hateful thugs.
From the ashes of betrayal
Comes me redefining myself.

No, No Regrets

You said I ruined our perfect lives when I left
And that you hope I'm filled
With nothing but regrets.
But all this time
I've been racking my brain,
For I can't recall
When a perfect life with you ever came.

Reconstruction

You Could Never Be Me

You scoffed, "That could never be me,"
Inserting yourself in my story for free.
Adding yourself as my heroic dual,
Rewriting my character as the village fool.
Oh, you've made yourself the lead in my story,
Bringing home all the fame and the glory.

My downfall is all it takes
To erase all your past mistakes.
For when I shared the chapter of my fall,
You suddenly became villainously tall.

You smirked, "My husband is not like that."
Now why the hell are you telling me that?
All this time, you've been comparing our choices,
Now you're rejoicing and lifting up voices.
Can't take your imaginary crown on your own,
Gotta kick me while I'm down to get your fake throne.

My demise is what's required
For your insecurities to retire.
You think you need to dim my light,
And somehow, yours will shine brilliantly bright?

You sighed, "My wife would never put up with him."
Way to go! Let me clap for your win!
Was this the perfect time to boost your echo?
Is your inability to read the room real or placebo?
White stardust falls on your wife every time;
So much perfection must be a crime.

My destruction solidifies your position,
Clarifying to me your egotistic disposition,
For somehow, this all became about you.
I wish your inconsiderate, selfish self would get a clue.

I smiled, "No, you could never be me."
A statement I made as I sipped on my tea.
For my experience helped me write my story,
And you became a peasant in it with no backstory.
I thought you would show me the same love and grace,
But in the end, you showed me your true face.

My true destiny was yet to be manifested.
Your hurtful words meant I was still being tested.
Whether ignorance or jealousy, you'll reap what you sow;
A judgmental mind keeps you stagnant and unable to grow.

Remnants of the Past Self

Hollow void enclosed in translucent shell,
A beautiful silhouette of what once dwelled.
The fading details of the sculptured mold
Embodies stories yearned to be told.

Radiant light dimmed by destructive fight
Once shined brightly for all men's sight.
Weathered by storms uncontrolled by nature,
Delicately moved from grasps of danger.

The reconstruction will require a balance,
Every substance will present a new challenge.
New beginnings will shape futuristic forms,
Inconsistent pieces will be buried deformed.

Mended cracks from remnants of time
Stood tall but were brought down in her prime.
Now evokes hope like a beacon,
Being re-released in twilight of Eden.

Like a phoenix, transformed from destruction,
Remnants of the self reside in reconstruction.
A new entity grows as the new self,
Reflection shows pieces of the past self.

Tears Turned Into Pearls

I turned my tears into pearls,
Each with chronological swirls.
One piece after another together,
Carefully linked like a precious treasure.

As I held up this tear-filled necklace,
An escaped tear showed me being reckless.
I smiled as I placed it back in its place,
For it is a lesson I now embrace.

I cannot change what was done,
Or all the trials I have run.
All that's left is what you now see.
My experiences have tailored me.

As I place this necklace around my neck,
I'm reminded each memory is a speck.
This necklace I now carry and control,
Shows that I am the master of my soul.

Thank you for reading my poems.

www.ingramcontent.com/pod-product-compliance
Lightning Source LLC
Chambersburg PA
CBHW060347050426
42449CB00011B/2860